the Peddler
and Other Domestic Matters

by Hollis Summers

POETRY

The Walks Near Athens

*Someone Else, Sixteen Poems About
    Other Children*

Seven Occasions

FICTION

City Limit

Brighten the Corner

The Weather of February

the
Peddler
and Other
Domestic Matters

by Hollis Summers

RUTGERS UNIVERSITY PRESS

New Brunswick, New Jersey

The author and publisher are grateful for permission to reprint poems which first appeared in the following periodicals:

The American Scholar: "Diano Marino to Aix en Provence" and "Sermon"; *The Christian Century:* "The State of Statues"; *The Colorado Quarterly:* "Bridge Freezes Before Road Surface"; *Kentucky Writing Four:* "Woodland"; *Epoch:* "Fraternity House"; *Impetus:* "The Old Man Opens His Eyes"; *The Minnesota Review:* "Inscription for the Back of a Parlor's Blind"; *New Mexico Quarterly:* "Lilies" and "The Gift"; *North American Review:* "The Lake Country"; *Ohio University Review:* "Décor," "Profert," "Love Poem," and "A Certain Poet Addresses His Reader"; *Page:* "To the Warrior's Mistress"; *Perspective:* "At the Wax Museum" and "The Performance"; *Poetry Northwest:* "The June Nuns" and "The Belonging"; *Prairie Schooner:* "Song to Be Attached," "The Maple Sugar Girls," and "The Traveler Hopes God Is Familiar with the Earth"; *Quarterly Review of Literature:* "Lines Not to Be Thought of"; *Saturday Review:* "The Velocipede," "The Progress," "Hickory Dickery," and "The Delivery"; *Southern Poetry Review:* "October 15, Cádiz"; *The Western Humanities Review:* "The Court Poet's Last Poem"; *Wormwood Review:* "Golden Anniversary"; *The Writer's Voice:* "Last Poem."

For Laura

Contents

II

I

THE PEDDLER

Finding the hotel was not the real problem,
Although hotels are difficult to find again,
Once you've thought them well left behind,
Once the wind has changed and snow has fallen,
Once you have bought a ticket to another town.

I found the right hotel, I am sure,
But I still did not recall the number of my room.
The clerk was busy at first, then disturbed:
"Somebody stole my records. My memory is poor,"
But he remembered me. He was sure he remembered.

We decided at last on the very top floor
And a mystic number, I remember a mystic number.
"We are right. I am sure there is no one there."
"We are right." "My apologies for my memory."
"My apologies." "The key?" "The key is there."

I joined a nun in the chromium elevator.
Her skin and wimple seemed made of each other.
She smiled as though we were familiar.
We soared quickly together.
She smiled as though we held a secret together.

And we were there, and she had disappeared,
And, behold, my numbered door.
I waited before the door, not from fear
I think, listening a while to the far
Sound of women singing. And then I entered.

The room was a thousand rooms I have departed:
The same draperies, the beds, the chairs, the mirrors;
And perhaps I spoke aloud, rushing to the dresser
("Thank God") where the suitcase waited undisturbed;
Perhaps I fell to my knees as if in prayer.

I do not mean to make too much of this story.
The suitcase held the articles I usually carry:
The same shaver, pajamas, a robe, slippers,
Three books I would logically admire,
And scrawled notes stuffed in a manila folder.

All of the notes I read in the darkening room,
Written in a hand almost or surely mine,
Naming journeys, listing living expenses.
In a dresser drawer I left the memorandums.
I am determined to believe the suitcase is my own.

CONCERNING REALITY

I have spent enough sleep
Dreaming fables to discover
All dreams happen
Among familiar places
Through long worn doors
In local swamps and parlors

Where figures keep
Appearing like parents or lovers
Or teachers or surgeons or children
Wearing the changeable faces
One has not bothered to care
Enough for.

I have dreamed enough to warn
Dreamers of the danger
Waiting for the dreamer who asks
Even once the identity
Of his dream men and women;
Inevitably the question
Dares to provide the answer.

I cannot speak of the turn
Of a mind among the strangers
Wearing each other's masques
Among a man's memory.
Who would dare question
These men and women
Perhaps houseled by a dreamer?

5

INITIATION, ANOTHER ONE

1.

First, in front of the bathroom mirror
Make a little ceremony
Of cutting the lock of your very own hair;
Chant names, including your own;
Then snip. You need not orate,
"I hereby dedicate this lock
To thunder." The snipping dedicates.
Place the hair in a series of boxes,
Three or five, preferably five,
Seal with a flourish and your monogram,
Slip on some clothes, and hide
The box in the careful hold you've planned
Beneath the garage or patio.
Anyone who finds the treasure
Will surely work his will on you.
Assure yourself your own possessor.

2.

With a little prayer and a simple fast
It is easy enough to incite a vision
And leave yourself oblivious
Enough to create a ghost—a man
Or beast or bird. I recommend
You conjure what is comfortable.
Myself, I always call a bird:
I fear them, they're available
And, after a bird-adventure,
The talk is considerably less.

Perhaps you will choose a tiger,
A woman, a lioness.

3.

Day possesses no mother.
Night is the mother of day.
Travel the night until you meet the vision.
Give a name to the bird or animal.
Talk with dark joy. Tell all
Secrets before you, eager, allow
Violence, before the vision swallows
You into the dark of its double jungle.
Accustom yourself to the darkness as you will.
Say your love. And then kill
The tiger, or the whippoorwill, or man.
Night is the mother of day.
Day possesses no mother.

4.

You will want to bring home your trophy,
Back to the suburbs of baths and patios.
You need never tell the neighbors why
Or how you killed the vision. Know
They also have experienced dark.
Invite them in. Say, "Company
Has come." Make speeches. Drink.
Shake paws or wings. Say,
"The name of the company is my name.
Let us play a company game."
They have done the same.
All of our hair is all the same.

5.
After the neighbors leave
Do not pretend to grieve.
Eat the trophy suddenly.

Say, "I have proved my love."
Say, "Bird, I gave you love."

TROUBADOUR

He came in carrying
His heart, all four chambers,
Bigger than a pear
Grown for an emperor,
Over his head, beating,
Beating, beating.

He greeted every lady
Seated in the chamber;
And then he sang his repertoire:
A song for Christmas, a song for September,
A song for May. A third of the company
Applauded each of his offerings.

But the princess, her hands held,
As if for prayer,
Before her breasts
Beating, applauded
Each of the three songs
Longer than any lady seated in the room.

Laughing, he began to juggle.
He juggled his heart the rest of the long afternoon.
But no one applauded.
He left the quiet room
Quietly, not quite undone,
His heart still over his head.

THE COURT POET'S LAST POEM

Once He bedded with a princess,
And once He killed in cold blood,
And once He prayed all night.
Reading from left to right,
As subjects, we inevitably delight
In such due process.

My own employment, unsettling,
Makes me honestly difficult.
He prayed. Then killed.
And then enjoyed the girl
From right to left, resulting
In His present job as King.

THE TRAVELER HOPES GOD IS
FAMILIAR WITH THE EARTH

Here from my seat within this air-cooled air
The road below moves casual as a river
Or a careless chalk mark, turning unreasonably
To peter out in a pasture or a mountain,

Leading, so far as I'm concerned, nowhere.
I do not worry about the mountain roads, never
Having lived with mountains. And I can see
The danger of pontification even when

My glasses cloud, particularly here.
Surely those suburban areas which recur
Like hiccoughs were planned by men to be held in fee
By men, carefully conscious of the nature of heaven.

Only incidentally does suburbia's pattern share
The shape of a fish's unswimming bones there
Where I, not at all incidentally, would be
If I weren't in flight again.

CABIN B—125

The steps do not fly endless down to Deck B
Not even if you start to descend from the top of the
  ship,
And still lower decks exist,
But do not count the flights; the floor of Deck B
Will say Deck B, there you will start to count;
To get to Cabin 125
Where you have paid to live
You will walk through seven possible compartments.

Seven chambers capable of being closed
Tighter than the doors of kings' vaults;
Seven wheels of silver metal
Wait beside the doors with arrows saying CLOSE
Or TURN; you must move turning close
Through the dim turned alley
Charted, named, Deck B;
You may turn around, but this is the deck you chose.

The railing there was designed for storms; rest if you
  will,
But not too long, TURN, the doors
Are not closed, like mirrors,
They are only framed, CLOSE, another traveler
Comes, see the other traveler appearing;
He does not wear your clothes; your room
Waits tight against the storm;
Rest, sleep, traveler, with nothing but turning to fear.

WORSHIP AT SEA

A Tourist Class Protestant I scrounged
Sufficient clothes for the classless Worship Service
Held for Protestants Only in the First Class Lounge.

We wrinkled sycophants assembled, less nervous
At the gathered storm than at the chance to move
Among fresh hallways dazzling as the Louvre.

The hymns proved highly unfamiliar,
Even to the First Class Stringed Quartette,
Even to Episcopalian worshipers;

All of us afloat faltered every note;
A man in a gown read a prayer of ancient origin;
Because of our nature there was no collection taken.

The Sermon, shouted above the air conditioning,
Loud as the waves, was delivered by a missionary man
Attired in a suit of blinding nylon,

Remembering all of his wicked youth in Evanston,
As well as his present problems in Barcelona;
He did not stop before the noon whistle.

All of us walked back to our proper quarters.
The sea stood, a crooked saucer,
Higher at the edges than where we wandered

Shriven back to our tourist berths.
There is no Sabbath on the sea,
Or every day is Sabbath.

HAMPTON COURT

A man in even partial armor requires
Heraldry for his identity
Without exposure; for the full armor,
Presently fashionable, heraldry
Proves itself as protective as the armor
And, equally vital, a decorative art
Allowing us to discuss design apart
From our passion for survival or power.

It is pleasant to dwell on the fine lines of a unicorn,
The colors and simple pattern of a flag,
The handsome clutter of the shield of any clan,
The sturdy figures that serve to guard the badges
Of soldiers, sailors, lords. Relish this falcon
Sufficiently bold and bright for a fluttering banner
And equally charming in ebony or china.
Regard this Yale, this Bull, this Dragon.

And yet it is simple to alter heraldic beasts
By changing extremities, as once, in this ordered garden
At the word of the man who ruled over Hampton
    Court,
The graceful leopards standing for Anne Boleyn
Became, at the hands of rather skillful artists,
Panthers to celebrate another woman
Whose son would play a lute and study Latin.
Mourn Anne Boleyn and her pretty leopards.

THE LAKE COUNTRY

Our sons did not approve of the rooms we chose
At Keswick. Mystic, they knew The Daffodils,
Down from the church and around the hill,
Waited clean and cheaper; they said a john
Should live on the floor you lived, not two flights down.

Our window, shaking its frame in the urgent wind,
Held an elderberry tree bowing
In front of the church, a smattering of houses;
Theirs held smoke and three wan mountains
Melting together like the center of winter.

The bar, windowless, boasted a mass of plastic
Flowers attracting wasps against the laws
Of logic, and a fire that flowed
Electric behind a scarlet cellophane disc
Coloring our faces and the faces of other tourists.

Beyond us, at Dove Cottage, not far beyond,
Rested a poet's hat, and some words he spelled,
A fan to shield him from the glare
Of a candle's light, an inkstand, a pen;
Cold rain fell on all the gardens.

"It's the worst summer any of us ever lived!"
The barmaid laughed as if confessing weather
Turned our situation better
Gathering our bones into a corporate chill.
Nobody mentioned Wordsworth, which was just as
    well.

16

DÉCOR

The two glass male robins
Cocking their slick identical heads
Assume the air of men who listen
For what may come from the milky bed
A china female hovers over
Among a flurry of pale petals;

The males pose as conceivable lovers;

The female hardly poses at all.

The table stands firm as an altar
Bearing the sound of waiting eggs
While real flies mount and falter
Arpeggio the table legs.

EFFIGIES AT WESTMINSTER

And so they lie as the only likenesses
Extant of the men and women they represent;
And so they illustrate medieval craft:
Cast bronze, covered with copper and gilt;
And so they have turned us all into pilgrims
Determined to get our money's worth from England.

But even the single figures lie uncomfortable,
Fallen, feet out, toes up, on impossible pillows;
And the couples, the men and women who officially
    loved. . . .

Do not consider the couples, the woman above, the
    man below.
They do not even pretend to sleep beneath
Above each other, lying tortured in their crowns.

No one could sleep in these human postures
Here, no more a triumph of civilization than prayer.

THE JUNE NUNS

Once in the very middle of June
At three o'clock in the afternoon
Five straight nuns marched
Across our beach and out to the end
Of our black rock jetty stretched
A thousand feet into the sea.

Four of the nuns with grace fluttered
Down to the rocks. The Mother Superior?
A Professor of Art? The chaperone?
Keeping a vow or managing structure?
Whoever, the other one stood alone
Against the green blue sky and sea.

We naturally spoke of their composition.
They came perhaps to brown their hands?
We considered ourselves the norm
Giving our members to sun and sand;
We were bemused by their uniforms
Beneath the sky beside the sea.

We have never learned the name of their order.
Yet long before that day was over
A gull began to patrol the rocks
Lifting and lowering all of our colors
Through careful waves of white and black
Above the sky, above the sea.

All afternoon we watched each other.
Not until late did the rocks gather
To march the jetty, to march the beach;
A slim moon, a white shadow
Hung sudden in the gull's reach
Of the bright sky above the dark sea.

DISCOVERY

At Pompeii you always meet the dead
Mingling with tourists in the Antiquarium,
Looking for the eggs and bread
They had not meant to leave behind,
Looking for pretties, pots and pans,
Their dogs and friends.
At dusk the dead go back to their gardens.

But once in Pompeii, at dusk, I
Alone alive I
Walked in a garden alive
And found blackberries
And picked and ate blackberries.

THE STATE OF STATUES

A pigeon seems to like to squat
On Saint Loyola's halo, Peter's shoulder,
The head of Baby Jesus, Mary's breast,
To top a cross or banner borne
By stone serious conquerors.

If you are feeling sufficiently phony
Declare: pigeons serve to turn
Weather wearied eyes from suns
Long burning; pigeons make stone
Remember life, enhancing composition.

A pigeon waddles around to turn
A work of art into something silly
Casual as a mind feebled
By experience. But, God in heaven,
How many people need to feed them.

CONFRONTATION

On an Angelico blue Sunday morning
We found an Italian ruin, an admirable forum
Recently walled (someone had found it before)
For strangers to circle and conjure the past.

We, the only strangers awake in Rome,
Carefully counted twenty-six cats:
Twelve slept, thirteen scratched,

And one stalked a green-gold prey
The nature of which we chose not to name
Since legends, like lizards, inhabit forums,
And this was not a conventional cat.

DIANO MARINO
TO AIX EN PROVENCE

Nobody has told me it is almost fall;
Always before I have been told;
My mother has said, "I hope the cold
Won't get the chrysanthemums,"
My wife: "The days are shorter,"
The children: "It's time for football,"
And all the while I have stood numb
In the sweating hot September summer.

It is difficult to tell a season away
From home alone in a cheap hotel;
But yesterday morning I knew well
Fall, standing on a balcony;
Below, in the quiet plaza, a man
Walked wearing a dark cape;
He did not look up at me,
But I left the hotel looking for the sun.

Yesterday at Nice, in the afternoon
The sun bathers arched their bodies
Above the rocks as if to hurry
Sun, although the air was warm;
I left my hostel without sleeping
To hasten to Aix whose name has been
All of my life a name for summer;
In Aix the trees stood weeping:

Plane leaves whispered the ground
By a king's statue. But today
The dead leaves have gone away.
Someone working the night has moved
The leaves away. I know trees
Shed often in summer at home.
But I, too, in autumn, have hidden
Evidence, sweeping fallen leaves.

SERMON

I wish to appear neither as evangel
Nor eccentric. However, I wish to appear.
And I am willing to run the risks involved;
Rejecting heads protected by hoods and veils,
Applauding faces worn by facing weather,
I admit nakedness and its rich necessity.

Still, I polish the bottoms of my shoes.

And I advocate such concern with invisible
Outward appearances, even to the painting of sepulchres
In abandoned foreign country cemeteries.
Although we rarely walk through air or water
At least at least we may walk in polished leather
On oil, and excrement, and tapestry.

THE SEA LADIES

The vast flowering women cling
To the railing, encouraging their voile berthas
To catch the full wind, winding

The air with their knotted laughter;
The paired ladies, buttoned to their chins
Walk mocking shadows of each other;

Some of the women rush from their cabins
To tell on stewards who have tried
To touch their thighs and make them sin;

While others ring for stewards to confide
Dark secrets; the very old
Sail sullen home to die

Considering the world a ship's hold;
And precocious tinies totter the lounges
Smearing marshmallow chocolates, bold

To whine desires in several languages.
The sirens, beautiful and young,
Pose at home to advertise our voyage.

THE BELONGING

Admire the dentist who wears dentures,
The spectacled oculist, the bald barber.
Distrust the amateur guitar player
Performing for only his private ears.
A tourist beachcomber pretends
To take a walk. He returns
From the unordered sea and sand
Wearing awkward pockets, undone
With all he has forsaken.
A professional carries a sack on his shoulder.
Music means more than its maker.

THE FOUNDING OF CORINTH

So, escaped from a poem, the black and white bird
Tried to lure us by stuttered flight
Away from the nest we had never guessed
Existed in all of Corinth.

We were trying only to build the city—
Apollo's temple gave us a start—
But the Spring of Peirene was full of stubble
And the Fountains of Glauce dry.

The bird called,
And, of course, we followed.

MYCENAE

These mountains wait fanciful
As any mountains made of papier-mâché,
Tall enough for receiving signals
From the sea or another century,
Bearing a hundred unpatterned levels
For pitching a field, an altar, a castle—
A beginning or an end—
Inhabited by choruses and colloquies
Or a man who speaks alone.

The crags rise for pushing over
And leaping from; the passes stand
Conscience-wide for departing conquerors
Conscience-thin for entering villains
Beneath a sky of every color
Meant to freeze or seduce lovers
And armies who dare the sun and moon.
This is a great country for murder
And mythology, but so are the flats of home.

OCTOBER 15, CÁDIZ

The sea is as usual: it spreads a fan
With a moving groove at the very rim
For ships to pose their silhouettes,
Look picturesque, and disappear.
But our beach is two miles long this year;
At low tide it is two blocks wide;
We live in the sea at high tide;
It is the beach that cares us, admitted tourists.

Whatever the tide, we walk through
A knotted cluster of ladies' shoes
And plastic dolls, disjointed—
Arms, hands, torsos, feet
Mocking our sense of moving complete
Down to the sea; but the sand is gold
And the waves move as waves were told
To move, as Neptune planned.

Here I would have created Neptune
If no one had ever told me about him:
The waves spray a chariot;
The manes of horses whip at their drivers;
Master tourists we ride far higher
Higher than the posturing boats
Bearing merely cargo floating
A groove behind our plastic parts.

Neither people nor haunting birds
Challenge our claims this stormed October,
Except at dawn when the sand is gray:
Two gulls, as big as eagles,
Patrol the beach for a little while
Followed by an old beachcomber
Who has never yet stopped to bother
What we forgot yesterday.

THE LIDLESS SLEEP

At night a parrot fish secretes,
Deep from the moon,
A mucus envelope for sleep,
A gelatin cocoon,
With a hole in front for breathing in;
For breathing out,
A hole behind the caudal fin.

I know about
The parrot fish.

              I have watched
A dozen ingenious lights,
Held by ingenious men in helmets,
Turn marine nights
To day.

            The men and lights record
The fish that daily flies
Through the dark sea scared,
But nightly lies
Helpless, through moons and sleep,
Despite his covering.

The men say the colonies of the reef
Adapted living
A million million years ago.

Dear God, I wish
To say I know I know
I speak of the parrot fish.

SHORE WINDS

Every man who has lived by the sea
Knows that the wind wears a woman's words
Listing the names of shells and birds
Through a quiet night, and the waves agree
To all of the names.
                  When the night is loud
The wind is a chorus that speaks no words;
No man can say what the women have said
Except the dead have been mourned.

THE UNPATHETIC FALLACY

Looking as old or older than boulders,
The young sandpipers hunch their shoulders

To take a feverish community walk
Clear from the land to the sea and back.

Looking as trivial as mechanized,
They dance out their pretty lies

Breathing above their patterning feet
Self-wound as athletes.

The young sandpipers pretend to be
Old lady poets flirting the sea

Whose waves long since have marked the sand
With penciled mountains running.

MONUMENT

Dressed in robes of white silk
The man and woman danced the hall
To tunes played by flutes and lutes
Before they lay to love a while
Beneath the moon lined like a map.
They gossiped and they slept.

This place is declared a monument
Since mosaic horses prance the wall.
But the window opens to the present scent
Of jasmine; the colored window still
Allows the moon on the marble floor.
Here lies the monument. Here.

TOWARD SANTIAGO

All of his elements, like God's, raged:
The weather was wretched, his bones ached;
And the men he rode with, average neighbors,
Had long turned savage.

What were they riding out to find?
A box that somebody said once held
A splinter of wood, a drop of blood,
And a couple of supper crumbs.

His knife was good, his stave was strong.
He could call himself mad without much pretending.
The cliffs seemed designed for falling down.
He could not turn back, with no place to turn.

So he bared his knife and coldly made
Seven slashes to turn the stave
Into flute enough for a man to play
As he rode.

THE GIFT

Somebody was bound to come before the announcement
Got out. It was a boy who entered, as wretched
As alone, hardly knowing the time of the year,
And never imagining noisy worshipers
Lined up, as if to have their pictures sketched
Or act in a rather pretty pageant.

He had decided he was through with sheep
And being tired and isolate and cold;
He had left his stupid flock at the edge of town
And scuttled dark to the stable near the Inn,
Hoping, at least, to warm a few of his bones,
At most, to give them full sleep.

The woman had borne her baby privately—
Her husband still searched for a friendly stranger;
The boy, afraid, but curious as afraid,
Waited until the woman, crying, made
A straw comfort in the stable's empty manger.
The boy heard the baby cry.

He knew that night, here, waited as a place
To know. He recorded the scene as well as he could,
The feel and sound and smell of straw and breath
Moving and being moved. Before he left
He looked hard at the child's dark head
And the way his eyes fitted his face.

He returned to his sheep at once, of course, to move
Among them, not remembering the face at all
Even while the sky bloomed song and light
Enough to shatter December and the very night.
Sleepless, time and again, he could never recall
The face, but considered love.

VOYAGE

When the middle of the sea moves black
No farther away than your own black hand
Pretend that the rim of the sea is land
Half close your eyes and name the land.

At home you will pay your dishonesty back,
Naming the habits of love perilous,
Calling the edge of horizons sea;
Many of us never guess
Where we have been led by the sea.

I think often of foolish Columbus.

THE PHOTOGRAPHER RETURNS

Our tired wives stood among the ruins,
Shouldering Hadrian's wall, supporting Tiryns,
Becoming Trajan's column, sucking in
Their stomachs to smile and smile another minute.

Wait. One more. Smile. Look different
Another minute. And acres of our dusty children
Fidgeted smile squints against the sun
Toward windmills, castles, guards, gardens.

We have held the smiles through winter and a screen
Blaming the camera for people we have never seen
Blaming the sun for places we have never been.

THE VELOCIPEDE

The day said November, the sky noon,
And that was the time I chose to ride
The velocipede with electric power
First owned by my father, then my sons,
A handsome vehicle of heather color,

A worthy machine, fully proved
By all my knowable generations
With trips to town and lakes and mountains
And places bearing no name but love.
I had never ridden the velocipede.

I did not recall I had never ridden.
But both of my sons and one of my father
Stood on the porch to watch me mount,
Shouting farewell as well as huzzah.
"Goodbye," I called. But I did not move.

The three men laughed and clutched each other.
"It's not plugged in," shouted my younger.
"Throw us the cord," shouted my older.
"We'll fix it up," roared my father.
The three lions roared and chortled together.

I had not noticed the cord before.
It was longer than cords for typewriters
Or electric fans or vacuum cleaners,
But not long enough to go to town
Much less love, or lakes, or mountains.

43

The motor started. The men had contrived
A clever extension from the front porch light.
"Let us know when you have arrived,"
They called together. "Come back alive."
They were not unfriendly, and noon shone bright.

"Where have you gone? How have you traveled?"
But no one could hear above the roar
Of the heaving motor. All the while
High in the cupola, a lamb, my mother,
Watched me riding around the block.

LAST POEM

It is safe to carry a queen bee
Naked in your naked hand.
It is unsafe to carry a stove

Lighted. Both danger and safety
Lie in carrying insurance. Stand
With these three truths to prove

Your place in natural history
And moral. The inquiring gods demand
Regular proof. It will behoove

You to know a queen when you see
One and yourself. Nature has planned;
She stings her kind, without love.

II

THOSE HOUSES, JANUARY, 6 P.M.

Those random houses crouch along the ridge
Eating bites from the sky even at noon,
Even in spring, like somewhere France, or Spain;
In winter, at dusk, with one dimension,
They organize the whole sky of Athens,
Ohio, wearing electric buttons
Or holes, as if they proved the leaning sun
Of somewhere thought and somewhere remembered.

SABBATH MORNING

By edict of the council of our town
The jailer's house has been torn down.
The jail has nothing to lean against
Except the white Sunday air
And the vague eyes of worshipers
Stopped by the wall that once shared
A side for evil, a side against.
The prisoners wait in another town
For their jailer's house to rise again.

High in the wind of the second floor
Stand two doors as heavy as doors
That lead to asylums, or vaults, or tombs.
But our local eyes, headed for prayer,
Are not prepared for the colored squares,
Green and pink and lavender,
Naming the walls of the jailer's rooms.

Sing the homeless jailer and the doors
That lead to space. Once, sing.

WOODLAND

Only three quiet children,
Two mothers, and one madman
Walk the morning here in this Monday Park
Where a rusted sun squints dark
Over this town, and businesses rush
Making up for Sunday and the hush
Of yesterday's ridiculous stillnesses
Hovering the air with angels and witches filled
With questions for everybody about the accident
Of love and its necessary deliberation.

DEVOTIONAL

You need not bother God with prayer
For the motorist who travels far
Among the stable ends of earth:
Tourist accidents occur
No more than twenty miles from home.

If you must engage in prayer,
Pray for the deliberate traveler
Who dares not leave his considered hearth
Or, daring, returns familiar
With another hearth he considered home.

Bless with care the ashes where
Fire burns, bless the fire;
Admit your own position of earth;
Name the man you pray for
Traveling among the dangers of home.

FEBRUARY 22, SNOW

Again the reasonable season brings
A white day in by its scruff
And lays it far and near enough
Against this window for reconsidering
Among the yard's familiar trappings

Left from fall and farther back,
Among the snow that falls, appointed
By weather men and aching joints,
Leaving the world of fact abstract
As thinking about the thought of thought.

But still I know the row of angels
Comprise the maple trees we planted
In ground not necessarily haunted;
The ghostly pointing sentinels
Were and are clothesline poles;

The chariot, a wheelbarrow,
The temple ruins, a pile of wood.
Within this morning I have stood
Understanding. I would not borrow
Truth and other sorrows.

The group of huddled headless men
Consists of box whose start we stole
Beneath the eyes of a guard's patrol
About the yard at Mount Vernon
Whose honest owner abandoned reason.

53

PROFERT

Agreed. As much as the next one
I am inordinately fond
Of naming complexes, my own

Included. Hostility wearing a label
Becomes, if not less hostile,
At least less painful.

We can sleep, having recorded
An engagement for lust or a firing squad,
Once the clock is set and wound.

But Oedipus really married his mother,
And Clytemnestra rejected Electra,
And Stephen really died a martyr.

BRIDGE FREEZES
BEFORE ROAD SURFACE

All of the Commencement speakers were right, Alice:
Life is a treadmill from Albany
At least as far as Syracuse and possibly
Farther and further. But there's no good in being

Despondent, Alice. You can make your way
Almost asleep through the identical miles
From Rest Stop to Rest Stop smiling
To smile at the identical waitress who serves

A single meal. Just because you've seen one
Doesn't mean you shouldn't smile again
At the carbon copied service station man
Serving his single fuel. Be comfortable

Knowing the exact location of lavatory,
Soap, and toilet, as well as where to purchase
Your anniversary cup and a joke in a package.
After all, you do not move singly, Alice.

55

INSCRIPTION FOR THE BACK
OF A PARLOR'S BLIND

Let us suggest that you abandon wrong
And right, along with unicorns, mah-jongg,

And dying of scarlet fever here where
Houseflies settle upon the sequined swatters,

And children drowse, and dogs snore during
Visiting hours heroically coupling;

Not even the breathing flies, or children, or dogs
Believe the blossoms blooming in catalogues

Without a timely stitch in their hearts or crotches.
Let us suggest you carefully do what you watch,

Go where you look, say what you're listening to,
While thinking you much, tipping our heads to you.

LINES NOT TO BE THOUGHT OF

You expect a nest to be a feathered cradle
Softer than sentimentality
To comfort the bodies of wriggling bare birds.

But big-headed kingfishers defy any parallel
With naked wriggling humanity.
They dig their nests, nescient of feathered words

In logical cliffs, close to feeding waters.
They line the holes with bone.
They feed their young, at first breath, fish.

Ignore the beauty of kingfisher sons and daughters
Who fly comfortably alone.
Please do not give tongue to your logical wish.

THE BROTHERHOOD

I have been around too long
Not to know everybody
Looks and acts like somebody
Else I used to correspond

With one of those days I lived
Assuming I was the only present
Tense with any correspondence
To prove my amative

Nature unaccountably novel.
Oh, those were the days when the whole
World fitted in a nutshell;
I did not name as miracle

A tree, or turning the world around;
I did not see the shadows cast
By the shapes of love held fast
In sight and sound.

I did not know a man could not
Remember the feel of skin.

THE OLD MAN OPENS HIS EYES

Other mornings I waked to summer
And a room full of yellow and green light.
Other mornings among the trembling colors
I rose sudden at the center
Of a world spiraling to focus,
Not remembering my appointments
Either with policemen or dentists.

The light trembles because I look through screens,
And eyelashes, and dreams left over. My sight
Arranges the light slowly to mean
Nothing except I have finished waking.
Perhaps I should not try to make much
Of an old man waking on a summer morning
Enchanted with waking on a summer morning.

THE DELIVERY

I promised to look out for the child while I wrapped
    the boxes.
He was unattractive, with glasses that magnified his eyes
Into no eyes, and a stinking breath, but I like children.
He kept coming in and out and in and asking questions.
He could not understand any of the arrangements.
I answered as well as I was able, all the while wrapping
    the boxes.

Most people do not understand the art of wrapping
    boxes.
These are particularly difficult. You not only place the
    first
Into the second, but the second into the third, with
    tape and string
More complicated than music or wallpaper. I do not
    like to boast
But I have proved myself adept at wrapping boxes.

I suspect the parents came for the child. I am reason-
    ably sure.
The vast boxes triple wallpaper the room, ordered as
    Bach.
I have filled out all the forms left by the messenger.
I feel reasonably sure I will be questioned.
I will answer the questions as well as I am able.
And then the boxes will go to the trucks.

GOLDEN ANNIVERSARY

Frightened and smiling she could not lift her wedding
    dress.
He did not consider trying
Although he recalled the evening together they lifted
    the dress
Frightened and smiling.

The children were strong. Together they made the dress
    perform
Antics and capers in front of the mirrors
And laughing the youngest bore from the attic the form
    whose form
Remained unaltered.

They dressed the form in the crowded mirrors. They
    helped her stand
Beside the man, and once more
The couple smiled behind the form with another stand
For the frightened photographers.

LILIES

Consider the varied illnesses of lilies
But concentrate please on the mosaic disease.
There lies your double trouble, gardener,
And knowing how lilies are supposed to appear.

I suggest you choose your planting space
In early spring, determining a place,
If difficult, both open and protected.
You'll wait for early fall, naturally, to bed

The bulbs, allowing them time to consider
Growth, surrounded with sand, attending moisture.
Then wait, with prayer and decomposed manure
Suspicious of the spectacle of their tentative flower,

Alert to destroy mottled plants with mottled leaves
        where virus
Lives, carried by an inconsiderate aphis,
Leaving leaves strange enough to possess
You with wonder, as dangerous for gardeners as desire.

NOTES FOR A MAN INVITED

When, finally, all of your colleagues have gathered
You may admire the weather, since any weather
May be championed some that day: proffer,
If you must, several scattered compliments
To their cookies and their flower arrangements;
Then study your watch as if you had an immediate
    appointment.

They will present the plaque. Accept it.
Glance at your name and date and tribute
Bitten into the conventional shield screwed as a gift
To the conventionally slick square of wood. Announce
Acceptance and leave, knowing they will be eased
A little only by a final act of final arrogance.

They know the walls of your house are long since taken
With real space and real prints and paintings
Chosen because you chose, as they have chosen,
The nature of the walls to become invisible
From being watched and ignored. Giddily fearful
The younger, only after your departure, can become
    comfortable.

A little while employed they cannot consider
Even the idea of retiring lovers or batsmen
Considering forward toward another space
Lying in directions unutterably undiscovered.
They are also unsure retiring ever means
Another word for grace, becoming another way of grace.

HICKORY DICKORY

I have never expected to find a bone in my cupboard,
Or pies equipped with plums and singing birds,

Or initialed commissioned cakes, gentlemen's eggs,
Hot or cold pease-porridge, or talking pigs;

I have no more waked among stair-wandering ganders,
Or sheep, or cats, or winds, or seated spiders,

Than I have set forth to Banbury Cross or the moon,
Following a King of France or a piper's son;

Or slept in a treetop, or a shoe, or a haycock;
But the mice race up and down the clock.

PRESCRIPTION FOR AUGIE

In order to endure the surprises of the merciful
And chaste, paint
Every room of your house a different color
And add saints

Free hand, drenched with golden halos,
Swathed in black
To decorate and bless your own going
And coming back

Having watched birds fight in air,
Enemy women kiss,
The faces of old gardeners looking at October
With happiness.

SONG TO BE ATTACHED

Decorate the carcass
Thread with amethyst
Stud the brow with topaz
Zircon for each wrist

Twist the breast with emerald
Diamond for the waist
Shining as a slogan
Carefully many-faced

Baste the thighs with sapphire
Brilliant as a phrase
Deck the bowels with ruby
Weave a garnet maze

Braise in precious ointment
Drench it if you will
Decorate the carcass
It is a carcass still.

THE EXCHANGE

The small tables started it: the tavern table
Removed itself from the upstairs hall
Clear to the front parlor where the butterfly
Stood; the butterfly ousted the gateleg;
The gateleg, the candlestand; the candlestand, the tav-
ern;
And then the other possessions joined in
Making highly unlikely arrangements:
A rocker at a table set for dinner
Where a bed had once seemed permanent.

We did not mention the phenomena to each other
Until our draperies, our clothes, indeed all of the furni-
ture
Left home to live with our hillside neighbors.
We said we were fortunate our friends' accessories
Fitted our house so well. We admitted everything is
movable.
The planting went next: the maples turned to apples;
The privet hedge replaced itself with laurel.
And then the pets: our Siamese for a mongrel.

But we endured, and glad I am we did.
After the conferences, the letters to the editors,
After all the loving and hating awkward words
We have all settled into our altered neighborhood.
And now, outside, a moon shines like a gold thimble
I remember, the first memory of all.
The house is determined to collect ourselves.
The hillside trembles.

DANGEROUS TOY DISCOVERED
LOCAL PURCHASERS WARNED!

If you bought a doll this season
Imported, yes, from Israel,
Produced, for unlikely reasons,
By a company named Love,

Despair. The doll is inflammable.
Take the doll from your child now.
If you sent dolls to other towns,
Recall the dolls now. Now

Tell all: do not dare to caress
The doll, do not burn.
The doll gives off a toxic gas.
Take it to the fire station.

Suspect all dolls now.
Firemen will dispose of dolls.
Even the light of a Christmas bulb
Will ignite, like love, the doll.

ONE MORE PIECE ABOUT ORPHEUS

Oh, yes, I know his voice quieted beasts,
And moved such immovables as rocks and trees
And got him into hell
After the death of mortal love
Who went under the name of Eurydice;

And he went under the world and found her,
And yes he felt and talked and cared
Too much even in hell,
Knowing no fool breaks rules
Or vows in hell. Yes, I am aware

Of the sexed-up Maenads who tore him up in pieces.
I once heard his caved head prophesy.
But I do not blame Apollo
For finally telling him to hell
With all the singing prophesying noise.

I resent our writing him hymns.
He proved his pieces, means through end.
He won after all
All over earth and hell,
And, after all, his lyre burns in heaven.

FOR A COUPLE OF TROUBLES

1.

In the field which only this morning lay
Brown and quiet as the sleep of a tired woman
Without a conscience, suddenly play
Or quarrel, or perhaps merely become,

At least a thousand birds and an equal number
Of cats. Not knowing whether sought
Or seeking, the field leaps cats and birds
Who lunge and plunge screaming caught

Among the waking bewildered air that sings
Boomeranging birds and cats, and keeps
Supplying birds and cats. As surprising as spring
Comes the waking consciousness of a woman's sleep.

2.

Season his venison
With calendula blossoms;

Spread his bread
With roses and asters;

Offer as wine
A glass of rain.

Some men learn innocence
After experience.

FOR THREE SPECIFIC FRIENDS

1.

If your hands were expertly severed
Above your wrists where you wear
Or wore, a watch, a bracelet;
If your hands were lighted and made to appear
Like human hands, or hands that hold
Fruit and jewels in a store window,
Glittering, intentionally partial;
If your hands were placed below
The scented folds of opaque curtains
Artfully hung to keep hidden
The acts of bloody cleavers and hatchets,
Who could tell whose hands from whose own?

2.

You can tell almost all in a poem.
Tears, semen, and bowel movements
Come precisely with fairly simple aids:
Color and consistency charts
Stapled to the wish to show and shout.

I also wish to show and shout,
Look at me, look here, look out
From where you read, considering the poems I need.
I am sorry I have been reared
Believing poems that said, "Look there."

3.

A poem is room enough to skin a cat in;
A poem is shaking a stick at a cat;
A poem is skinning a cat more ways than one.

71

THE MAPLE SUGAR GIRLS
AT MAPLE INN

"We are the Maple Sugar Girls;
With lips of ruby and teeth of pearls
We smile beneath our clustered curls,
And we will marry lords and earls;
Our mothers look at us askancey,
For we are elegant and fancy,
We are bright and right romancey,
We are Eunice, Avis, Nancy."

As elegant as pictures of magazine ladies
Attending a doctor or thinking of sin,
They stand near the shade of the maple trees
And smile provisional smiles at the Inn
Whose layers of porches still circle to see
A mountain and a meadow. In the watered sun
The ladies consider how far through a map
And a clock and blood they have come. Undone
With the consideration are these three:
Nancy, the dreamer, and Avis, the madcap,
And Eunice, the remarkably practical one.

Here, enduring scheduled culture
Their terrible mothers and heat rashes,
In tighter bodies, once, they burned
Mottoes in birch about the lure
Of Mother Nature. Here they learned
To embroider dots and dashes
On dresser scarves. And here they wrought
Beaded flowers and leaves wriggling
For headbands. They pillow fought,
Read Elinor Glyn and Louisa Alcott,
And dreamed of knights, giggling.

But most of the summer they shared the view
With the meadow that watched the Inn, asking
Each other, "What is this similar to?"
Of the Inn, or Life Itself basking
In a unified sun. Feeling pretty,
Nancy said, "An enchanted castle."
"It's a wedding cake," Avis said,
Feeling ethereal. Feeling witty,
Eunice said, "A wooden hotel."
They said to each other, "How truly true!"
Pledging allegiance until they were dead.

"Once we spent time."
Yes. "And the meadow was larger then."
Yes, the dark trees grow,
And meadows contract with time when
You aren't looking. "We made up a rhyme
About ourselves." Yes. "We know
The song." And each knows all the parts,
Mad, dreaming, practical;
The Maple Sugar Girls, again
And still, laughing, cross their hearts
Not to die, and enter Maple.

("We are the Maple Sugar Girls;
With lips of ruby and teeth of pearls
We smile beneath our clustered curls . . .")

In this hotel, or castle, or cake
By the small meadow, the other guests
Will move through summer to praise
The song of Nancy, and Eunice, and Avis.
The Maple Sugar Girls will keep
The Inn from moving past the murmur
Of the dark trees, out of summer.

Bless Nancy, Avis, Eunice.

THE FRATERNITY HOUSE

The fraternity house of the Pi Kappa Alphas
Once was a funeral home
Where the loudest sounds were the purple buzzes
Of lavender telephones
Calling above the orchid whispers
Of an organ's electric bowels
And the hiccoughs of trembling mothers and sisters
Thinking long vowels.

When the cooperative brothers of the brotherhood
Moved to the mortuary
They whispered and tiptoed as they thought they should
Before the registry
Where visiting mourners had signed in on
To prove they bled.
Then somebody belched and dropped an urn,
And the boys adjusted.

The parlors are marvelous, of course, for dancing
And preferable to parked cars
For making almost love and chancing
After hours.
And the shed at the rear of the Grecian mansion
Where victims once were prepared
To meet their God for final scansion
Now, thoroughly aired,

Serves for building homecoming floats
Protected from rain and wind
Assured of winning the judges' votes
For enduring past their stand.
And bells and hiccoughs and organs quiet
Still with a new trophy
And the loving oversight of night
Upon young bodies.

THE HEROINE

She was a twin, the ninth child,
Cried in her mother's womb,
Appeared at noon on Good Friday
Wearing an admirable extra finger
And a caul that looked like embroidery.

She had the extra finger removed,
Refused to chant a spell,
Prescribe a simple, escape herself,
Or rearrange the patterns of love.

Strew with palms the way of this practical fool.

LOVE POEM

1.

And all spring this room has waited
While we have slept in a distant bed
Full of no sky and no shadows
Dancing Byzantium on the ceiling?

But we had heard the tree beginning
Song under black snow below
No moon shining perilous.
No room possesses us.

2.

We have moved across this floor younger
Tonight than twenty years ago; mirrors
And other eyes prove us incapable
Of missing any music; and even while
No music plays our feet still become
The music, and our bodies make the room
A mirrored illustration for perspective
Where lines stretch infinite.
We need not necessarily remember
The burden of our bodies left us awkward
Once, for we have moved with grace
Wearing our lined faces.

3.

I would no more celebrate the nature
Of marriage
Than fortune;

But once, aloud, I wish to say
We have lived today
Quietly;

We have moved from first light
Through noon
Into night;

We have lived all day
Without apology,
Without one lie.

SHE SENDS THEM
TO HAVE A PICTURE TAKEN

Surrounded by the debacle of a department store
His son and he, in line, moved closer
Toward the presence of the lady photographer
Who would photograph anybody's child for a dollar.
He was embarrassed among the women and their
    daughters.

His son refused to share his hand or conversation,
Also grunting against all soft feminine discipline
Called love by mothers. The men itched with chagrin
Considering the horror of vanity curled for a bargain,
Considering generalities about men and women.

Yet, committed, they pressed their flesh toward the
    event
Of a present face frozen into a document, opulent
And permanent, of all their relations, an ornament
For the study a little while, and then subsequent
Attic burial. They waited, neither bystanding nor inno-
    cent.

And we reached the presence. She stood in black before
    us
And smiled at a rubber clown. She did not discuss
Pictures or dollars, and my son laughed in focus,
And so did I, louder than the clown, utterly joyous
Or mad, totally involved and anonymous.

FIRST LESSON

If you objective painters must attempt
Religious subjects, and you must,
I know you must, let me suggest
You restrict yourselves to portraits of minor saints
And small blessed objects: be leery of themes
Already proved involving group scenes
Such as Calvary and the Last Judgment.

The great ones often failed at Nativities—
Study your Christmas cards: a seated committee
Vapid as tedious, and the child greedy
To open his presents, looking at least thirteen
And uncomfortably like your nephew in Toledo,
Old enough to be working daily at the Temple—
Better to paint at a lamb or a tangerine.

I know everything is lost in composition
To be replaced, perhaps, by something fine
But different. We must remember these differences.
Consider the Cross, Ascension or Descension:
Mary and the other waiters tend
To pose at grief. Composition makes demands.
Some of the friends stand around like an audience

For television instead of the words, "I thirst,"
And somebody turns to watch the photographer.
Even the *Pietàs* end up often only pretty:
She could be looking down at an outsized pet,
Or a cousin who snatches a drunken nap on her knees,
Or an intricate piece of Pastrana tapestry
Depicting a culture she has never read about.

All right. I know you will never be content
With saints and other tokens. Go ahead. Start,
Admitting composition. But try an Annunciation first.
No one can prove how either of the figures felt.
Go on. Consider the postures of Mary and the angel.
At least your failure will be graceful;
The subject makes the air inevitably bright.

THE PERFORMANCE

I still dream some nights that I sing
For a small fee to ladies' groups
Who relish songs the movies sang
When they and sound were young.
My voice is elegant and rings
Us all together. I stoop
A bow and see my father waiting
Waxen among the moth hands
Applauding. He always drives me home
From the engagement. I do not comprehend
His waxed face. I say, "You're driving."
He always says, "I understand."

THE PROGRESS

A bumblebee circles the flower world
The sun circles a daffodil
Down the round hill
A boy runs the sun
While the sky holds no horizon.

    I don't step in chewing gum much any more,
    And almost everybody has stopped getting killed
    At railroad crossings, and WALK signs make it easier
    If longer to get across streets, and marigolds
    Bloom lovelier than ever,

    While the morning sun keeps on calling
    And coffee still tastes comfort
    And the children tell what happened at school
    And we go out and we invite company in
    And evening falls.

A fat cardinal sits in the catalpa tree
Among gray runic branches
Under a sky the color of pencil marks
Erased. The cardinal flies
And all the words appear.

THE STUDY OF HISTORY

Upon this selfsame sofa
Quietly my grandfather

Slept away at least
Ten thousand pieces

Of ten thousand suns
Naming afternoon

To wake refreshed
To face the rest

Of men who also served
Good Queen Victoria;

He slept as I shall surely
Sleep, as I have slept

Differently governed
By certain sovereigns

Waking among the long
Ungoverned evenings

Under this same cover
Upon this selfsame sofa.

85

AT THE WAX MUSEUM

Here where Gary Cooper's figure stands
Holding truth enough to fool his mother,
Where a fresh carnation and Gloria Swanson
Bloom equally fresh, and the James Brothers,
Guns alert, measure Gina's body,
Here I would speak my knowledge of busied works,
Surrounded by Caesar, Cortez, Laurel, Hardy,
Considering such idle matters as life and art.

The tenses merge, accompanied by air and water,
Earth, fire, proving John Kennedy
And the presence of Isaac Watts.
Henry VIII eats. Hannah feeds
Her son near Newton, Luther, Al Capone,
Moses, Joan. . . . I would name them all
Whose urgent hair has been precisely counted
As naturally as counted starlings fall.

Once I picked a rose from my own garden
And placed it within a lovely woman's hand;
Undone at the blood of my act with a casual thorn,
I considered the rose and the woman dead;
But the living woman laughed beside the bed
Of yellow roses, pushing back her hair;
"Hurry, take the picture," the woman said.
Oh praise God presently, everywhere.